"Here, we have a once-in-a-generation debut cc  of a book than to be solid and to be company to the Little Caesars Arena, from Cadieux to ' loving stare as hot girls turn up and exit the l streams. This is not a debut, this is one Bad Mother.

I've rarely felt momentum like this, each poem sequenced with intimacy and an aversion for simple answers. Audacity as mandatory for survival. Survival as mandatory for sovereignty of self and city. We're all accounted for. The dress suits us. The garment, like the soul it amplifies, cannot be ruined. A city and its library branches like a heart and its chambers. The book has us dressed. Its smooth meter inflicts the flyest ramifications on her image-thick stanzas. With these poems, we know where we are and we know who we love. We know the stakes but the music refuses to abandon us. Poems are so back! They never left. The Midwest is here to stay. It never ever left. Detroit is our conscience and our level. *Good Dress* is for Rogers' Detroit what 'The Bean Eaters' was for Brooks' Bronzeville.

Long have my bookshelves begged for a book as self-possessed, as incendiary as *Good Dress*. As a Black woman, I am affirmed and joyfully goaded. As a poet and student, I am impressed and seated! And as a human with a yearning ass soul, I am gratefully in debt. Brittany Rogers is already a legend and the first of a new kind of poet for whom truth is a posture of both the line and the mouth. A poet come to wake us up for good."

—Angel Nafis,
author of *Black Girl Mansion*

"Through lush imagery, slick syntax, elegant diction, and play with form, Brittany Rogers crafts generous and keenly observant poetry. *Good Dress* knows Detroit and all its migrations: the East Sidedness of its own language; its Down South tell-it-like-it-is because I love you and mean it. Night deer in the pastoral of empty house lots, the heaven of a corner deli that knows you by your name. These poems force us to consider what we mean when we say home, and who gets to tell that story. Exploring gentrification, queer eroticism, motherhood, and church-girl blues, Brittany Rogers makes it her business to insist we look at it all—the catastrophe and the beauty—and leave none of its wisdom behind. This self-assured, dazzling debut has a story to tell. And says it with its chest, its whole mouth."

—Arieka Foreman,
author of *Salt Body Shimmer*

"*Good Dress* clothes us in a challenging and bold extravagance—Detroit-flavored, wide-awake in a time of social upheaval, changing self-perceptions, and complicated relationships with religion and other people. Even when 'grief lays her hand / on my cheek,' the speaker in these poems recognizes 'how the body becomes an altar.' What we put on our bodies eschews sin and shame when grounded in choice. Femmes enter a night out elementally engaged—bodies 'sweating, edges ribboned under / summer's breath'—in their beauty and search for pleasure, for belonging to oneself and a nurturing Black community. 'Can't nobody outdo us,' Brittany Rogers writes. Indeed. Rogers' electric debut enfolds us in what we didn't know we needed to understand about how we can move in the world, to dance and roller skate and cry, to imagine ourselves adorned passionately with life."

—Khadijah Queen,
author of *Anodyne*

"Brittany Rogers' *Good Dress* is an audacious, grounded, and generous debut. Rogers is a poet who brings us in, brings us close. These poems double and split, ask who to blame and who to absolve, sing elegy and extravagance, turn always toward home."

—Donika Kelly,
author of *The Renunciations*

"*Good Dress* is an electric and atmospheric debut. Rogers constructs a lyrically pulsing Detroit in which its people and their dreams, desires, and hopes are made unapologetically legible. This collection captures the spirit of resilience and singularity through powerfully visceral verse, while painting a vivid portrait of living beyond categorization. On these pages, Rogers does the damn thing by deftly lifting the veil and demanding the beauty of people and places often deemed invisible be seen, attended to, and felt."

—Airea D. Matthews,
author of *Bread and Circus*

"'Perhaps I have always been / a greedy thing, god / of too much,' and aren't we lucky for this good appetite's growl reverberating throughout Brittany Rogers' toothsome *Good Dress*? A catechism worrying the questions of goodness, these poems enact good form broken bad—brace yourself for what Rogers pulls off in the sonnet crown 'Good Ground.' And who is this ground good enough for, this book ponders in anti-pastorals on gentrification, in queer odes to Detroit libraries, and in the clinically empty spaces of medical forms. My goodness, I have waited so long for this collection."

—Tommye Blount,
author of *Fantasia for the Man in Blue*

Good Dress

poems

Brittany Rogers

TIN HOUSE / PORTLAND, OREGON

First US Edition 2024
Printed in the United States of America

EPIGRAPH CREDITS: Excerpt from *Song of Solomon* by Toni
Morrison, copyright ©1977 by Toni Morrison. Used by permission of
Alfred A. Knopf, an imprint of the Knopf Doubleday Publishing
Group, a division of Penguin Random House LLC. All rights reserved. | Excerpt
from *Some of Us Did Not Die: Selected Essays* by June Jordan, copyright ©2002.
Reprinted by permission of Civitas Books, an imprint of Hachette Book Group, Inc.

Manufacturing by Kingery Printing Company
Interior design by Beth Steidle

Library of Congress Cataloging-in-Publication Data

Names: Rogers, Brittany, 1987– author.
Title: Good dress : poems / Brittany Rogers.
Description: First US edition. | Portland, Oregon : Tin House, 2024.
Identifiers: LCCN 2024025400 | ISBN 9781959030836 (paperback) |
ISBN 9781959030904 (ebook)
Subjects: LCGFT: Poetry.
Classification: LCC PS3618.O45646 G66 2024
LC record available at https://lccn.loc.gov/2024025400

Tin House
2617 NW Thurman Street, Portland, OR 97210
www.tinhouse.com

DISTRIBUTED BY W. W. NORTON & COMPANY
1 2 3 4 5 6 7 8 9 0

For Gloria Jean Young, my whole heart, who loved me enough for this life and the next.

"She was fierce in the presence of death,
heroic even, as she was at no other time. Its
threat gave her direction, clarity, audacity."
—TONI MORRISON

"And what shall we do, we who did not die?"
—JUNE JORDAN

CONTENTS

●

GOOD DRESS

MONEY

after watching the video by Cardi B
after Tiana Clark

I, too, want
to walk in   the bank
brazen   to rain
dollars over my friends'
asses   fund any pleasure
                we want

I want enough
money for men   to cover
        they eyes when
I walk in   the room   enough
that no one reaches
for my waist   without asking

I want to perch
straight-backed
and haughty   pat my pussy
        shoulder roll

                        damn, I'm fine

                        I was born to flex

        it's not really about   the money

                who would I have been
                        had my family kept
        the land   we owned
before the factory buyout

before we stopped   scraping change together
to keep the farm
I never got to step foot on

I don't want   to be rich
I want enough coin
to relax
to spoil

my damn self   to tend to the baby
gasping and rooting   for milk
without worrying
about ruining

my good dress

THIS TIME, POSTPARTUM

dresses herself
in a long cerulean
housecoat, cotton
hem dusting her ankles,
as she saunters in
without checking
to see if I'm fit
for company.

She kicks her slippers
off at the door
before she moves
about my kitchen,
whipping up a stew
so thick with roots
I'll be eating
off it for days.

INTAKE FORM

Please have this form completed before your first session.

What concerns bring you to couples counseling?

> *There has been no abuse in this relationship. No infidelity (that I know of). No (hard) drugs. He has never hurt me "that way," if that's what you asking.*

Are there past issues I should know about?

> *I was hurt ~~once~~, maybe. My mama left his ass right in the nick of time. There was my ex and that man ~~and her and the~~ I don't want to discuss this issue. I do not want to confront my abuser(s).*

What are the strengths of your relationship?

> *It's fine. I'm stable. My sex drive recovered. My kinks are not important for this discussion. I'm not guilty ~~anymore~~.*

What are you hoping to get out of these sessions?

> *My mama threatened to have my hymen checked after complaints of a stomachache. I know what you're going to say: Maybe that's why I chose the ~~people~~ men I fucked. Trollop. Maybe it was all spiteful. Unnecessary. My man says he loves me incessantly. I believe he thinks he means it. My mama says she just ain't want me to inherit her mistakes but I am already twice married. If he at the store five minutes too long, I think he ain't coming home.*
>
> *When he says "I miss you," I ask, "are you sure?"*

In an alternate version of this story
I grow up in Denver, Colorado, fenced in

by calcareous mountains and thread-thin air. Who might
I have become had we driven eighteen hours overnight to flee

the Red Zone, Chiron lighting the sky, Detroit's bass chasing behind?
I imagine Denver homes are large. Ivy clings to the wall

like sap. I imagine I could have walked to school unguarded, no knife
pressed to my ankle in fresh Js my mama wouldn't buy in the City.

Once the factories stripped the grass of its green, she was willing to leave
her mama on Jane Street and my aunties scattered from Cadieux to Van Dyke.

A diamond band convinced her to stay, but she models
what could still become of me: slips and stockings,

subdivisions, propriety. I could have run when I had the chance
but I'm a daughter of the East Side, that old girl set in her ways.

I grew a mouth like the grown men in my hood. Bouquet of tattoos
across my shoulders. Where brown hair was, a field of watercolors.

ELEGY

I wish I could say we bonded
during those visits I begged for,

but there is not much I remember
of weekends at my father's house.

Missing my favorite cartoons, too secular
for his other children to view.

The thick leather belt he threatened to take
to everyone under *his* roof, even the wife who

cooked every meal and kept the house
and birthed the kids back-to-back.

On Friday nights, he drove us
to prayer service. The pastor named

us wicked, destined for hell's hot hand.
Each week, the congregation widened

their fire-washed throats and wailed
so long the service outlasted the sun.

Each time, I fell asleep
waiting to be taken

home, the pews the softest part
of that small room, crowded

with bodies laid out at the altar.

Before the borrowed library card
became my new identity, I stole—
Zane novels tucked into Guess jeans,
something like guilt pebbled
in my belly. I never got caught.
Not there. Not in the park, or behind
that old church. Sprawling, sneaking vine.
All seven sins, and alive.
This is not a confessional, yet
the shelves watch me fill my hands
with possibilities. At night, I read.
Beneath thin covers, my fingers
flip, touch, imagine. My tongue replaces
each fictional lover's name with hers.

HUNTING HOURS

I walked everywhere that summer
and everywhere   there were men
making a game of their lust.

The chorus of catcalls licked my back
as I passed by, hips tender, swaying
like too-tall grass.

Fooled them. Most girls shy
away. I glutton. I devour.
I do not wait to be made a meal of.

I plucked the first boy from his porch.
Then the next. The next.
And   Him, too.

I left—hands stuffed with
their strands of hair, hickeys red ants
lining my neck. There was no one

at home to ask how or why
I would do such an unladylike thing.
Things.

Don't you see?
No one *took* me
this time.

PAULING BLOOD

Whenever my aunt recounts the tale,
she says she should have known—
muttering about Pauling blood,
our hard heads, soft behinds.
She told me and my cousin to stop running
in and out, wasting her good air.
When we grabbed the skates,
she forbade us from putting them on
until we made it off the front porch.
Of course, we said okay—knew to play
obedient, hide behind the tiny lie. Of course,
we galloped down the inside stairwell,
the leather itching a hole in the center
of our hands, so greedy we were to slide
them on. We know this part
of the tale by heart: the skates were on our feet
before the screen door slammed behind us.
I remember creeping down first, slow
as an old watch. Holding my breath
as my cousin inched toward the sidewalk.
So, you see, I was watching when her right leg flew
from beneath her on the third step. We both knew
her arm was broken before her elbow split clean
as wishbone, before my aunt heard her scream.

SELF-PORTRAIT AS DETROIT PUBLIC LIBRARY,
FRANKLIN BRANCH

No one wants to be blamed
for the chipped bricks
lining our exterior, or the sparse
garden, too stubborn to stand
straight and salute the sky.
They look past our outdated software—
our sagging shelves stuffed
with last decade's books.
We reach our arms across
the circulation desk and ask
for more than they have given us.
The state points its finger at the city;
the city points its fingers
toward the schools.
The school says "you're a smart girl,
use your problem-
solving skills."
Their jobs done, they leave us
with nothing.

DOIN' TOO MUCH

Ice Cam, Little Caesars Arena, January 2022

Kash Doll so Detroit
she throws herself
a Pistons-themed baby shower,
makes a museum of balloons
and basketballs and gold and gold
and fans call her gaudy. Tacky.
Twitter says a Detroit nigga
is just an Alabama nigga with Buffs.
Rappers gifted our governor a pair,
gratitude for the year
she dared keep our city from dying.
Outsiders didn't call her what they call *us*
for wearing sunglasses in a city
where we are the only light.
They say *ghetto* and mean migration.
They say *Detroit, stand up*, and we raise our wrists
like shot glasses. Toast to us in our colored
minks. In our Cartiers. Necks swaddled
in brick-thick chains. It ain't a flex
if he ain't wearing at least two and a Jesus
piece. If his watch ain't
thick as firewood.
What's love if your face isn't encased
in a necklace long as spite?
There are things worse than extravagance.
They all know our names.

DETROIT PUBLIC LIBRARY, FRANKLIN BRANCH:
EXPLANATION OF DEBT

To Whom It May Concern,

I came here so often ███████████████ knew me by my whole government name. Always by myself, lonely as a dream. I never asked for assistance. No need. I combed the dust-kissed shelves with the precision of a beautician's hands, looking for the cover ███████████████████. So close they could be . . . I could be. This is not about ██████ who kissed me in the vestibule of ████████. I couldn't return your books.

Not without being honest about ████████████████████████████████. You all should really consider some restrictions. Thick black ropes. An alarm that caws when minors approach. Anything to keep me from ████████ in that damp corner while the radiator hummed her low, uneven tune. I didn't bother with embarrassment. Maybe I was never a child. I did more than hold. And after, I snuck the books, all those books, to the dumpster and didn't consider at all what I might owe.

I LOST MY VIRGINITY AFTER MAKING A PACT ───────

He didn't notice my polished toes
how carefully I shaved;
the thong—neon, lace—I stole from Eastland;

He looked proud at his damp mismatched sheets
kept asking, *You feel me? It's good, right*;
My cousins fulfilled the pact first;

warned my skin would shred like thin fabric
I braced myself, waiting to slick a river for him

I didn't feel

my doe legs smoothed with cocoa butter;
Missy blasting *I don't want no one minute man*;
You couldn't tell me I wasn't a woman now;

red tide puddled in the middle of the bed;
My pussy didn't dance like the rappers vowed;
they swore I'd feel every pulse and jump

the second he spread me open;
instead, my hips and belly cemented like bricks

anything at all.

Granny promises again to buy us a wedding present—
a grill to host the family on summer holidays.

In this family, it's the women who grill. I coulda learned by now
had I paid attention when she took me to the ballparks:

Battle Creek on weekends, Jayne Field most afternoons.
The fellas swarmed her food stand like bees, willing

to pay the premium for chops or Polish sausage—hot dogs if their wallet
was switch thin that week. My granny tongs Midas-touched: meat smoked

tender as a goodnight kiss. I gathered with the girls learning
the Cry Baby in the parking lot, flat hips ironed

against sticky asphalt, thrusting,
popping the ass that I did not yet have.

I missed the important steps—lighting the charcoal, brining the ribs,
tricks to keep the kerosene's lick off the finished meal.

Now holidays come and neither of us can cook
her meat the way she likes. She would offer to teach me

again, hardheaded as I am, but dementia won't let her
fix her tongue to tell me how.

MY FATHER TRIED

I loved the water before
my father tried
to teach me
to swim—prodded—
no, tossed—no,
shoved me
into the pool at the Y.
I can say now
that I asked him
not to. I have never
liked being pushed;
he has never enjoyed
being refused.

Then, I thought I hated him.
His unsanctioned
fists, thick with force,
presidents of nothing
but themselves.
I emerged from the shallow
end choking, unrepentant
backslider tricked into baptism.
See, the chlorine.
See, my tongue bleached
white, so stiff
you could fold it
neatly in half.

I told him I would never
forgive him. I lied.
I can't forgive him
for that either—making a liar

out of me. Even now,
he is blocked everywhere
but where it counts,
his name stuck to the roof
of my mouth like tar.

PROGRESS NOTES

Week of ██████████

The patient pops off
every session.
Has yet to soothe her
hot head, tender
her slick lips.
Every day, a blowup.
She checks her seat
for blood. It is always
a wound with this one:
can't get to the cut
with all the wet
around it.
I prescribe antidepressants.
Stimulants. Redirection.
Picture your happy place.
I believe she has abandoned her plan
for treatment.
She stands to leave
and springs a leak.
Before she makes it
to the door,
a new trail of red.

SELF-PORTRAIT AS PAULING'S MARKET
ON LYCASTE AND VERNOR, CIRCA 1980S

Here, we break bread
and sell it.
Jar the pickles, pig feet,
penny candy. Here,
we manna. Miracle.
Make potatoes, rice,
and a pound of chicken
a whole week's worth
of meals. Careful:
the counter is guarded by
Mean Jean's children;
there will be
no forgiveness
for liars or thieves.
Ask anyone
about the last man
who walked through
these aisles sticky-
fingered.
Pauling blood,
every one
of them.
Ornery.
Watching
the door.

DETROIT PASTORAL

Who knows why
the deer choose
Chatham Street
to gather, but I drive
by the corner
lot, and there they
huddle—
glass-eyed
majesty.

We're not supposed
to see wildlife here
where sirens spin the night
air its own soundtrack.
Someone shouts
you hear that
and *that* could be
anything. Lock
your doors.

This block gap-toothed,
fickle. Field of yellow grass.
Field of soiled Pampers
and beer bottles.
Food desert,
but they graze anyhow.
Whole herd of heads
dipped so low I almost
climb out my car to kneel.

328 MACOMB

in honor of Elizabeth Denison Forth

They certainly have the imagination. Not a swarm
of maple trees, miles before you reach the river?

Not a field of pansies, puckered, awaiting
a passerby's kiss? Not even a row of brass benches,

a resting place for those weary of walking downtown?
A statue that the city will forget to appoint someone

to clean? The dignity of her fossilized home? No.
Of everything that could have been, there is just

a parking lot, potholes waiting to chew your tire
down to the gristle. Every Friday someone stumbles across

the asphalt, cackling and unaware. No one knows who runs
the joint. They charge a flat ten-dollar fee for entry.

SELECT THE MOST APPROPRIATE ANSWER

Considering the last four weeks, how often have you:

	Ratings				
	Never	Rarely	Sometimes	Most Days	Nearly Every Day
Been interested in your usual hobbies or activities	○	○	○	○	○
Felt down, tired, or exhausted	○	○	○	○	○
Been unable to complete the responsibilities of your job as a result of feeling down, tired, or exhausted	○	○	○	○	○
Practiced self-care (a bubble bath or kid-free errand)	○	○	○	○	○
Been so sad or exhausted that your spouse or children have seen you cry	○	○	○	○	○
Spent money you did not have on a material item that you did not need	○	○	○	○	○
Blocked an immediate family member or close friend	○	○	○	○	○
Neglected your body (no kink, tattoos, or piercings)	○	○	○	○	○
Questioned your version of events after being questioned by a family member, colleague, or friend	○	○	○	○	○
Formed ulcers, fibroids, cysts, or had other gastrointestinal issues	○	○	○	○	○
Considered that these "symptoms" may only exist in your head	○	○	○	○	○
Been harmed by another person (not including institutions or systems)	○	○	○	○	○
Found yourself calling for your grandmother	○	○	○	○	○
Woke up and said "fuck all this"	○	○	○	○	○
Had a visible breakdown (please attach documentation)	○	○	○	○	○

FLO MILLI SHIT

after Angel Nafis

Girl   you know you
    Black!
       Chocolate   Hey! CHOCOLATE!
Don't feel bad I like 'em
    Black

       Asphalt
         Africa
             Midnight
    Black
You brave   wearing that   yellow
Girl   you know
    you Black

Charcoal   Cocoa   Coffee
    Black
My homie said hey   SIKKEEEEE
    he like caramel
Girls   It's okay though   I like 'em
    Black!

Where you from   No really   Too
    Black
For that   platinum blond
Whew! You know you
    Black!

You giving   it up   Burnt that
    Black

Sweet juice   Birthing hips   Plum
Nipples   I bet   Yeah   I like 'em
Black

The Black Brittany
Oh   so you don't hear me   calling you
I know you
          Black   but the ass fat
Chocolate!
                    Slowdown!
                              I like 'em Black

ICE CAM, LITTLE CAESARS ARENA, JANUARY 2022

*That Pistons ice cam is some of the wildest shit I've ever
seen, do they not rob niggas in Detroit?! I would cover my
face and run if there was ever an ice cam in [   ]*

—TWITTER USER

When the ice cam turns wide-eyed
toward our section, we do what we must:
curl a thumb under the Cuban
link and lift high as praise.

No one is untouchable.
Not even you, pleading for us to quiet
our jewels cackling throughout
the stadium. Strip bare

our pinkies, wrists, chests—
for whose gaze? Those thirsty
for our throats and what they take
to be wealth? Your problem is

our nerve, thick as tobacco smoke.
You wish we'd get rid of it.
We know. We know.
The gold is just a cover.

30

GOOD GROUND

Before I was born, my kin
owned things: A corner store.
Two-family flats. Good ground.
We grew round fruit,
thick bark. Lost it all
and no one calls to explain
how. The living let lies fall
from salt-slick tongues.

*Not grown enough. Don't recall. Who told
you?* I comb through the obituaries
but they, too, lie closemouthed.
Maybe death is the only truth.
I keep trying to come home;
everywhere I'm from is theory.

Everywhere I'm from is theory.
I gather a bouquet of maps
and mark: *We Were Here.* Under
the factory. In front of that old
Catholic church. Where the eggshell
house was torn out the frame—
yes, there, under the freeway's
thin ankles.

My husband and I buy a house
on the West Side. Paint the dining
room tangerine. Walk to the park,
ballooned with barbecue, blunts, laughter—
oh, the laughter floating bubble-thick.
You gotta be from here to get the joke.

It's not funny, but it is. *They* done put—
of all things—a cocktail bar
at the corner of my granny's old block,
where her once-house now sits
desiccated and fragile.
How long has it been since I flew
from the garage roof, soaked
my bruise in her old claw-foot tub?

Can I tell you a secret? That house—
I didn't want it. Not then. I wanted everything
stainless. Forgive me for needing
land that I was the first
to walk on. I already belong
to them, all of them.

Daughter of all of them.
Daughter of hymns and riots.
Daughter of the remnants
after flames licked the whole town.
Granny says *we got people* down
in Georgia, the Carolinas, Alabama. She makes
me take their first and last
names, last rumored locations.

Good girl-child, but I lie
when I vow to visit
while in town. Instead, I workshop.
Craft talk. Fellowship. Buy books.
How do I look South for the living
when I last took the trip for the dead?

All I remember of the trip down South
is Detroit's frozen arms shoving
our minivan, full and cranky, all
the way to Orangeburg. I want to say
it was a good service—that my great-
grandfather's body *looked nice*, his hands
waxy like well-tended fig leaves.
Before we put him in the ground,

what looked like a snake sprang
from the yard of our distant kin.
I can't picture the casket, but I still
hear my cousin's howl of laughter
so loud the magnolias shook.
Look at us: so city, spooked by grass.

Look at me: so city that I won't consider
leaving though winter grips my neck
with its blue, blue fingers each November.
Ain't no rest here, but why should I give up
my house, my aunties up the way, my church
on every corner? My Black folks,
my hallelujahs, my makeshift cousins,
my *gatdamn*—can't nobody outdo us.

We all know New Detroit
got sticky fingers. See how it stole
Cass Corridor? Midtown?
Belle Isle? The family's market?
My granny's house? Is this the bounty
her mama migrated for?

Her mama migrated here
after the first riot, years before
the second. I plead for stories
about Georgia: *What made y'all flee?*
Would you ever fly off and leave us?
She swears she's here to stay,
but the only honesty is death.
She reminds me she'll meet the Lord

one of these days. I don't want Him
to have her. Forgive me my blasphemy.
She's where I get my ornery tongue. She is where
I get my everything. You expect me
to give that up? I belong to this line
of daughters; before I was born, her kin.

CONFIDENTIALITY AND PRIVACY POLICY

The law protects the relationship between a client and a psychotherapist, and information cannot be disclosed without written permission.

Exceptions include:

- Suspected child abuse or dependent adult or elder abuse.
- If a client is threatening serious bodily harm to another person.
- If a client intends to harm themself.

With the exception of certain specific situations as described above, you have the absolute right to the confidentiality of your therapy. I cannot and will not tell anyone else what you have told me, or even that you are in therapy with me, without your prior permission.

I have read the disclosure statement and I have had sufficient time to ask any questions that I needed to. After reading the Disclosure Statement, I understand my responsibilities as a client. I understand that therapy can have potential emotional risks and after carefully considering the risks and benefits of therapy I agree to undertake therapy with ██████████████.

See below

Signature of patient

If I am one Black girl, I am all of us. Keeper of my mama's name and my mama's business, which stays in my mama's house. I left a long time ago, but some stains don't come out in the wash.

That's halfway why I'm here. My ornery grief. My lust and all its backtalk. I listen. Adorn. Push back. My nerve barks order in my direction, and my answer is always yes. Not a damn thing belongs to me but me. Even this shame was passed down—a too-large mink, draped over my shoulders. Every secret wants to preserve my mama's heart. And ain't that sad, grown as I am? Grown as I am.

THE YEAR THEY LEFT EVERYONE TO DIE

for Ajanaé

Fact: I feared I would not live
through that last labor. Fact: sometimes
(more than half the days—no,
nearly every day) anxiety licks my face
with its wild, irrational thirst, and I feel
its damp threat for hours. My therapist
gave me a worksheet to track
my catastrophic thinking, but I am valid
this time, contracting, watching
my blood pressure leap. You FaceTime
from Ohio to monitor how they place
the IV, the epidural, the flat hospital pillow
behind my humid back. Fact: you
are the first call I make after, at three a.m.,
over the sound of newborn lungs learning
themselves. I promise, I did not make you
drive the three hours back home to tend
to my dry nipples, my everything bleeding,
my hair, unbound, sparking at the roots.
Some things take hours to dig through.
What has a lover seen that you have not?
Can I tell them you sat me down and parted
and greased and twisted? That for a week,
all I ate was made by your hands?

FLO MILLI SHIT

I ordered the Fenty
months before the last birth,
after the miscarriage drug
grief by its mangy neck
and left the remains—leaky, foul,
ruining my clean floor.

I tell myself I earned
the impractical—sex,
sheer panties, splurging—as
I rush to get my purse,
stepping over the bills
pooled at the front door.

The sun nudges the curtains
open, draws me close
enough to kiss her heat.
I put on the lace, midday,
and pose—thigh cocked
over milk-drunk sheets.

ODE TO MY MAMA AND "THE PURPLE DRESS," CIRCA 1992–1993

In this picture,   my mama know she fine
lavender sweater clinging   all her curves sitting right.
Glory be her exposed thigh   earrings licking her shoulders
her hand a cocked smirk at her hip.

I squint when I see lavender sequins   fitting her curves like lingerie.
Teenaged me couldn't picture my mama a woman   dressed to pull
her hand a cocked smirk at her hip   cabernet-colored lip
curved like a fishhook   dragging men behind her.

Before this picture I didn't see her as *just* a woman
though I know she must have been   those hips
curved like a fishhook   dragging men behind her.
We don't discuss who she was   before children

though I know   she belonged to herself   once.
She says she is too old to wear miniskirts, run the streets   now
that we wore her down. We don't discuss who she was before.
What picture will I show my kids to prove   I still got it

once I'm tricked into thinking I'm too old for miniskirts,
the glory of exposed thighs, large hoops? I imagine
my children   squinting at old photos   proof that I was a woman
before them, thinking in this picture   *my mama know she fine.*

"ROCK THE BOAT" IS A SONG ABOUT STRAPPING

after m. mick powell

according to my Pastor, who I, like a fool,
mistook for the voice of God, calling me by name.

Of course, "strapping" was too vulgar a term for her holy
mouth, though she called Aaliyah everything but her name,

and me, *funny*, for watching a woman dancing with women.
Their bodies whisper-close. Not a man in sight. I want to name

that I'm embarrassed to tell you this: I let the knife
of her stare stop my hips from rocking. Nodded as she named

my litany of sins. Unnatural. Ungodly.
In my own home, I changed the channel. There is a name

for the type of lie I told with my mouth closed. For what I pretended
to not know as clearly as my own name.

DETROIT PUBLIC LIBRARY, KNAPP BRANCH:
OVERDUE NOTICE

Dear patron,

The items listed in this email are now 21 days overdue. In 14 days, if the items have not been returned, they will be assumed to be lost, and your library account will be billed for the total replacement cost of the items. Please return the items at your earliest convenience.

OVERDUE ITEM	DUE DATE
Addicted. [Zane]. ISBN 0967460174	05-01-2005
Best Bisexual Women's Erotica. [Bruce, Cara]. ISBN 1573441341	05-01-2005
Best Lesbian Erotica 2003. [Taormino, Tristan]. ISBN 1573448893	05-01-2005
Between Lovers. [Dickey, Eric Jerome]. ISBN 0525946039	05-01-2005
Black Silk: A Collection of African American Erotica. [Powers, Retha]. ISBN 0446676918	05-01-2005
Cheaters. [Dickey, Eric Jerome]. ISBN 0451203003	05-08-2005
Delta of Venus. [Anaïs Nin]. ISBN 0151246564	05-08-2005
Girls' Guide to Getting It On: Everything You'll Ever Need to Know about Great Sex. [Everett, Flic]. ISBN 0007124147	05-12-2005
G-Spot: An Urban Erotic Tale. [Noire]. ISBN 0345477219	05-01-2005
Invisible Life: A Novel. [Harris, E. Lynn]. ISBN 0385469683	05-08-2005
Lickin' License II: More Sex, More Saga. [Intelligent Allah]. ISBN 0981854575	05-12-2005
Mom, Dad. I'm Gay: How Families Negotiate Coming Out. [Savin-Williams, Ritch C.]. ISBN 1557987416	05-08-2005
No More Sheets: The Truth about Sex. [Bynum, Juanita]. ISBN 1562291483	05-01-2005
Shame On It All: A Novel. [Zane]. ISBN 0967460123	05-08-2005

BEDSIDE BAPTIST

When done right, the final
ringing run of "Total Praise"
flings my clay arms
so wide the sun could jump
straight through.

From my laptop, I watch
Fantasia put on a concert
in her living room. She draws
out that last *Amen*—
the note sucked pearl-clean,
so full my chest grows thick
with water lilies.

I'm not fit for the Lord's
house: crop top
bonnet, boy shorts.
Lust-drunk. Giddy
off my own perfume.
I last wore a slip
when we lived

at the church three nights
a week. Back then,
I shamed my mother
when I wore jeans. Refused
the baptismal pool. Fell

asleep in the back pews,
in the lap of a girl I was
too close to. I don't miss
the thin rows of wood, their
stiff frowning faces.

At home, I am my own
priest. I offer my shrill
praise. Proud.
Loud. So rowdy,
He runs in
to see about me.

MY MAMA'S MAMA LIVES ALONE, THOUGH PERHAPS IT IS TIME:

She swears no one has been by to sit
a spell, forgets the croquettes until
the alarm over the stove bellows
its broken note. My mother is a travel agent:
sells Alabama, blade by blade, through FaceTime.
Look, my garden. All this yard.
These empty rooms, and a walk-in closet.
There is a way to stay

independent. My mother was grown
enough to move cross-country, but oh,
how the pleas rip through her throat
controlled as Mahalia's contralto
when she requests her mama leave
the last place she can claim *hers, all hers.*

BLACKOUT, AUGUST 2003, DETROIT

*It was one of the biggest power outages that the U.S.
ever saw. At first, people were worried it was an act
of terrorism, but when the blackout was confirmed
as merely a power outage, the mood shifted.*

—*MICHIGAN RADIO NEWSROOM*

The grills turn up. Somebody speakers
serenade all our porches, and we jam,
smoke-soaked and lawless, all open
hormones and this powerless field.
What is it about the end of the world,
makes you think you are owed
an explanation? From God. From
your mama. From the boy who ghosted
months ago, when the air became
more steam than breeze, his number
still memorized and half-dialed each evening.
You would chase him down, make him answer
to you while the streetlights are silent,
but this block, this city, don't know
how to tell us apart in the daylight—
done swallowed whole bodies before
this night, ripe for disappearing.
First, the "man" of the house next door
swept clean off his mama's porch.
Maria, a dandelion blown away
from the passenger seat of her new man's
custom Cutlass. My city give a fuck
about the proper order of things. She love
a malfunction. All them downed
wires. Mirrors broken in the street.

Our minivan sat on stolen bricks
by thieves kind enough to leave the metal
skeleton stripped in the driveway. This block
hormone-swole, smelling herself. There is
no law. Sometimes, in May, it snows.

Says he never seen a Black[1] girl
with hair *this* bright[2] before.
He a lie. No child born in the '90s missed
Lil' Kim in "Crush On You,"
a vision: *Queen Bee, undressed*
in a bra, all see through.
I begged to get my hair coiffed,
colored, monochromatic.
Wanted to be crushed on—
my lily-soft skin finally
lusted after[3]—I'm a lie.

I wanted to lust
after Kim, brazen, like the boys[4]
on my block; to grab
at my crotch, eyes howling
at my tv screen, hoping to catch
a glimpse of what lay
beneath her apple-red mink
bikini, without my mother
peeking over my shoulder
asking what I was staring at
so dangon hard.

---

1 Deep dark, dark enough to be insulted for it; not light-skinned; not caramel.

2 Forbidden; unnatural; any shade other than 4, 1A, or 1B.

3 Being lusted after *by men* was never the problem.

4 Boys can't help it, after all.

Testify: it's true, what they say
of our winter, her rotten mouth
foul, flighty temper.
All season, we want to be
anywhere but here. And yet, we obey
February's shrill whistle. Sit.
Stay. Roll over. Stay.
There are colder winds.
In some states, sunlight is a myth
whispered by folks who are from
not there. But what of it? What,
when there are cities
where the soil is soft
year-round, the sun chirping
and kind each morning.
The sun will not rise early—yet
today may be the day to unplug
the sunlamps, glaring at each other
from their corners of the room.
Wade in. Light the candles
on the dresser; the vanity;
the nightstand. Fling
open the curtains. Wide.
Wider.

*Major flooding occurred in the lower levels of the Detroit
Public Library–Main Library, during the torrential
rain storm on June 25, 2021. Every room and area of the
lower levels were impacted by the relentless downpour.*

—*DETROIT FREE PRESS*

The sky broke that summer,
salt-swept the city, collapsed
the freeway's movement.
Some say they were cursed

anyway, those man-made roads
that crashed straight through
the parts of town
built by Black migrants.

This is not a poem about the freeways,
or the way the city emptied
when *we* arrived,
but if those roads filled like a pitcher,

we should have known
what would become
of the basements,
even Burton, monument

that it is. Was.
Photocopied maps.
Obituaries.
Property deeds.

Records of whole families
floating in a pool
of their own waste.

ELEGY FOR REMEMBERING

The penicillin shot took
my grandmother's memory.
She's always been allergic

to needles, flowers, perfume;
whatever might make her well.
Time so janky, wheel's whirring

in reverse. *Who is at the door?*
At random, she recites
old addresses. Sends me

to the gas station with enough quarters
to play the numbers:
3661 when she dream-walks

to Beaconsfield; 1832 on the mornings
she wakes up decades ago, staring
at the cemetery across the street.

I don't visit like I should.
These kids, that school, this man.
"Self-care." The thirty-minute drive

across 94. Granny ask why it take so long
though we both know the East Side don't do
shortcuts. She's a child in awe

when I call, swoons
Girl, the Lord put you on
my heart and here you are.

On days when the penicillin
is a pair of dice rattling through
her brain, she calls me

by my mama's name: *Kat, you remember*
when? Back before your daddy died?
When we was on Lycaste?

I play along. Imagine Lycaste
predemolition. Granny not yet widowed.
My mother, someone's child.

Three years now since she up
and moved to Alabama. I'm not sure
which one of us Granny believes

is on the phone. *When you gone come*
see about your old girl?
Bring your tail on home.

I only needed to go
to the altar once, but no one
stopped me, tiny bride
lured by the organ's sweet
brown tongue.
I beat the choir's last hum
every service
Living, He loved me
giddy off Communion wine;
my twig arms stretched
toward the patched roof
where I imagined God
sat, watching me kneel for prayer—
again, again—in last week's stockings.
Perhaps I have always been
a greedy thing, god
of too much. I swallow
and swallow, snake-throated
miracle. *Oh, how He loves me.*
I know. I begged for it.

TO TENDERNESS

for Mars

Your green, growing hands,
your symphony of plants—
ZZ; Zora; Baldwin; Audre—

stretching for the sun's
applause. What does not bloom
before your attention?

You notice everything:
My moods tilting scales.
Which hymn will soothe

during the ride home.
How I like my food (not touching),
my drinks (brown and sweet),

my compliments (layered
like cologne). Have you noticed?
How much taller I am

seated next to you? Smiling
at the sky like the clouds
will return the favor.

HONEY-DO LIST, WEEK 34 OF PREGNANCY

*I'm sorry to ask. Please bleach the baseboards; stock up on Kotex With Wings; store
the diapers; buy 4 packs of Kanekalon from the back wall of the beauty store.*

The OB predicts *any day now*. Stress sharpens my nerves; picks me
apart at the seams. Hasn't catastrophe taught me that hope cannot be stored?

My father wept when he saw me in my wedding dress. What is it to love
a man most moved by watching you vow to obey? What store-

house sold me the language of asking too much? The church's scriptures?
My father's nag? My own trained tongue, all its backtalk stored

away? My therapist says I ignore my needs until they grow sores.
Maybe my bloodline did not make my brain sick. I am a storage

unit, stuffed with dismantled furniture. I don't mean to hoard.
Science says our cells cling to, pass down whatever we store.

I force my mouth to pour: *Can you? I need.* Before I ask, there you are, mercy-
soaked tongue: *Brittany, do you need me to grab anything from the store?*

ALL THE REASONS I'VE SAID YES

A dare. A bet, no money
on the line. Never for money,
though I should have. Not for
what I would call money, but
certainly for knowing I would be
good enough to get a bill paid.
Day care covered. The fridge filled.

Because I was mad at the other
one. Because _____ didn't
answer the phone. Because,
when I get anxious, all my nerves
coil tornado tight. See how fast
they spin? We don't get tornadoes
in Detroit—at least not yet.
In school, we still practice
the drill twice a year. Practice.
So much practice. I wasn't sure that
I would ever make it to you.

LYCASTE STREET AND VERNOR HIGHWAY RESPOND
TO THE CHRYSLER PLANT BEING BUILT

Summer has arrived
and there are no children
to shriek in front yards,
chase behind the ice-cream truck
careful to avoid the cracks
across our old corner.

Our corner store is gone.
Our apartment buildings—gone.
The small brick homes lining Lycaste
like a picket fence—all gone.

The only view from here
is what folks migrate
across state lines for.
They all know the plants
pay well—
clear the college debts,
earn the family a home
on the "good" side of town
where the houses have not yet
been demolished, the sky free
of factory air.

Wouldn't be no *good*
side if we hadn't been
here, our land
widespread, so ripe
y'all paid good money
to pull us out
by the roots.

Every Monday, folks swarm your doors
like yellow jackets,
dressed in their Sunday best
hoping for hiring papers; willing
to work machinery until their hands
are brick-rough, backs hunched over
for years postretirement.

There is no movement on the block
these days—only the screech
of machinery, the grinding
of hot metal.
Still no one driving by can say
the perks ain't plentiful—
that Chrysler employees
don't clock out
looking pleased
with their honest day's work.

Now that grief lays her hand
on my cheek; curves into my chest—
lover; child; a ghost bearing
the face of my grandmother.
Now that we are close enough to greet by first name,
I look out at the sea of jewelry and see
how a game can be a memorial,
how the body becomes an altar.
Rows and rows of gold pendants
thick as fists, gripping portraits of beloveds.
This grief heavy, wrapped around our throats.
Oh, how it makes us casket-sharp,
so flashy the camera
can't bear to look away.

SELF-PORTRAIT AS K&G DELI OFF WARREN AND CONNER

The boundaries are clear: a handwritten sign on the door warns: *Please do not ask for loose cigarettes. We do not sell any loose cigarettes at all. Please show Proper I.D. Thank you.*

Anything can belong to you if you ask right. Fuzzy peach candy. Gummy bears in Hawaiian colors. All 2 for a dollar. Here, you can smell like cheap perfume, jasmine incense, or body oil—

your choice. Hennessy and Hpnotiq. Alizé and Absolut. The type of drank put hair on your chest. Only in this store, on this corner: a copper jug of Lucky Nites Golden Liqueur

40 proof. We'll teach you to glutton without sin. Mac and Cheese. Rice and Gravy. Sponge-thick lemon pound cake. Blood-moon rib tips. Every type of chicken you aching for.

Come: wash, shave, drape in weed-adorned fitteds and tall tees, pack tomorrow's lunch, change the Pamper, bleach the sink, scrub the soiled carpet. There is a choir of Black women waiting

for you at the door. Hair did, nails did—waiting to get you right. There is no rush. We'll be here damn near all night.

TREATMENT PLAN

Please answer the following questions to the best of your ability.
Your responses will be used to develop a care plan that meets your therapeutic goals.

Who is on your care team?

> *Some people have only one great love. I am a lucky girl. All my lovers been gentle-handed. I am an octopus. I heart and heart and heart. All hands, touch, come here. I call out to my beloveds and they sing back here I am.*

When do you feel most like yourself?

> *My legs splayed open, spread wide as a kiss. Tied down. Bound. My tongue soaked. My mouth full. Pressed so close to another, their sweat becomes my own.*

How do you know when you're safe?

> *I carry a teddy bear when I travel. Whatever I don't see disappears. Certain foods can't touch. Most smells sour my stomach. For one year straight, the same meal each morning. I like what I like. I hate what I don't.*
>
> *Who cares enough to make my plate so that I can eat from it? Who can predict what I won't notice, and bring it to my attention?*

Is there anything else that you wish to disclose?

> *I belong to me. I belong to me.*

FLO MILLI SHIT

84-inch box braids, tips twirling across the floor. grown woman
red lips, nails, panties. R&B night at RollerCade. *all you couples
report to the skate floor.* slow grind. slow roll. white shellac on
the toes pre-spring. brown liquor's sting, vines spreading down
my throat. a baby at 20, all mine. another, another. yes, working
poor. my third curls into me; tender, ball of yarn. no more. tubes
snipped at the roots. I choose. I don't need to check in with my
husband. today, I am not working. no—not sick time, a personal
day off. instead of meeting the deadline, I take a nap.

THROWBACK NIGHT, MIDWAY SKATING RINK

I ignore the kids' slinky arms. The dishes. They daddy. Tonight
I rush to the rink with my best friend, her fingers locked into mine.

The sun dipped already, but we sweating, edges ribboned under
summer's breath. I forget to take pictures, but trust. We fine.

Out after dark, awestruck at our own grown. Downtown
ain't looked like ours since *they* landed on Woodward and mined,

hollowed the center to erect a high-rise. Joke's on them.
Everybody here Black and in love and my,

don't we know how to reclaim what's ours. We on beat with it.
Look how our thighs obey: backward, glide, turn, slow whine.

The DJ cuts to "Cupid Shuffle" and even on skates, we hustle. Our necks,
tilted bottles: laughter splashing and messy. Oh, how I mined

for this belonging, scythe swinging, searching for my name. So busy
hiding from selfish, I had dropped damn near everything that was mine.

I AM TOO PRETTY FOR THIS

after Ross Gay, after Gwendolyn Brooks

—a spell I cast
when shame opens
its lying mouth
and calls me out my name:
the once-lover swung his fist;
my front door padlocked,
belongings sprawled
on the patchy lawn.
Check 'n Go knows me by name,
and so does the nail salon.
I should be embarrassed
by how I preen
before beauty's lap.
I know what they say of the hiss
of vanity, how it holds me
back from heaven. I know also
how grief folds my voice
into its back pocket. Don't think
me dramatic. People have died
touch-starved, penniless.
I will not settle for anything
less than sunflowers. In every room, a vase full
of their ornate faces, bone-straight backs.
Everything keeping me alive is the most
beautiful. Every day's color is yellow.

Notes

The poem "Money" is written after Tiana Clark's poem "BBHMM."

The title of the poem "Money" is borrowed from the song "Money" by rapper Cardi B. "Money" is an ekphrasis that was written after watching the music video, which was produced by Jora Frantzis. This poem also borrows the lines *"damn, I'm fine"* and *"I was born to flex"* from the song.

The Detroit Public Library system is the largest library system in the state of Michigan, and is one of the cultural hubs in Detroit. The first Detroit public library opened for service on March 25, 1865. As of 2024, there are twenty-one branches in addition to the main branch located in downtown Detroit. The Detroit Public Library is a publicly funded, independent, municipal corporation; it is currently governed by the Detroit Public Library Commission, who are appointed by the Detroit Public Schools Board of Education. The library system has been at the center of numerous controversies, including city takeovers, mass closures, fraud, tax discrepancies, and financial crisis.

The title of the poem "Doin' Too Much" is borrowed from the song "Doin Too Much" by rapper Kash Doll.

In the poem "My Father Tried," the phrase "presidents of nothing" is borrowed from Aracelis Girmay's line "She was my mother, after all, / & president of nothing." found in her poem "Cooley High, Fifth Estrangement."

Elizabeth "Lisette" Denison Forth was the first Black landowner in the United States. Although she was born into slavery in Michigan, and spent much of her life enslaved in Detroit, she and her family escaped to Canada, and returned as free people years later. Forth worked for the Biddle family in Detroit and was a shrewd investor; she eventually earned enough money to purchase land—first in Pontiac, and later in Detroit. She also invested in numerous businesses. In 1854, Forth moved to Paris with the Biddles, and returned over a decade later. She lived out her last ten years in Detroit as a free woman. When she passed, she left a considerable amount of money to the Saint James Protestant Episcopal Church with the goal of enabling them to construct a chapel where all people, regardless of race or class status, could worship together. Forth is buried in Detroit's historic Elmwood Cemetery.

"Flo Milli Shit" is written after Angel Nafis' poem titled "Nostrand Avenue, Brooklyn." The title phrase is the tagline of rapper Flo Milli.

The Ice Cam (also known as the Swag Cam) is a feature at the Detroit Piston's basketball games. Similar to the "Kiss Cam," the camera scans the crowd during the game; however, instead of kissing, sports fans are expected to flash their jewelry or extravagant outfits. The Ice Cam was introduced in 2021, when general manager Troy Weaver and Vice President of Brand and Marketing Strategy Tyrel Kirkham wanted the Detroit Pistons organization to more deeply reflect the culture of Detroit.

"'Rock The Boat' is a Song about Strapping" is written after m. mick powell's poem "thesis: *Rock the Boat* is a song about strapping, if for no other reason than." It is also an ekphrasis written after the music video for "Rock The Boat." The music video was directed by Hype Williams, while the song was recorded by singer Aaliyah.

The epigraph for "Blackout, August 2003, Detroit" was taken from the article "Ten years after the great northeast blackout of 2003," written by Mark Brush from *Michigan Radio Newsroom*.

The poem "Ol' Dude at the Gas Station Think He Flirtin'" references the music video for "Crush On You," which was recorded by rapper Lil' Kim, featuring rapper Lil' Cease. The video was directed by Lance "Un" Rivera.

The epigraph for "Detroit Public Library, Burton Historical Collection" was taken from the *Detroit Free Press* article "Detroit Main Library, Symphony and more see temporary closures due to storm damage," written by Kimberly P. Mitchell.

"I Am Too Pretty for This" is written after Ross Gay's poem "Sorrow Is Not My Name," as well as Gwendolyn Brooks' poem "To the Young Who Want to Die."

Credits

Many thanks to the following journals in which these poems, sometimes in different forms or with different titles, originally appeared:

Four Way Review, "Detroit Pastoral"

Hopkins Review, "Benediction, Israel Baptist Church"
and "Ice Cam, Little Caesars Arena, February 2023"

Indiana Review, "Doin' Too Much"

Kresge Arts Detroit, "Good Ground" and "Detroit Public
Library, Chandler Park Branch: Erotic Fiction Section"

Metro Times, "Aubade for the Changing Season"

Mississippi Review, "Money"

The Poet Lore, "Treatment Plan"

Prairie Schooner, "Throwback Night, Midway
Skating Rink" and "Upbringing"

Room Object Anthology, "Self-Portrait as
K&G Deli off Warren and Conner"

Underbelly Magazine, "Ice Cam, Little
Caesars Arena, January 2022"

Acknowledgments

I'm honored to have such a rich community, to be writing alongside so many brilliant and thoughtful folks. Whether you have edited first drafts, stayed up coworking, offered affirmations, or been a source of inspiration, much gratitude to the following: Jo'Van O'Neal, Rodrick Minor, Kirwyn Sutherland, Jassmine Parks, LaShaun "Phoenix" Moore Kotoran, Aurielle Marie, Nicole Homer, Raych Jackson, Britteney Black Rose Kapri, Kush Thompson, Franny Choi, Danez Smith, Natasha T. Miller, Kelsey Ronan, Cat Batsios, Alise Alousi, Nandi Comer, Taylor Byas, Dior, Imani Davis, Mathias Pitts, Tianna Bratcher, Rachel McKibbens, Alafia Nicole Sessions, Jae'lah Glenn, Aja Allante, Kennedy Byrd, Miona Short, Penda Mbaye Z. Smith, Isha Camara, LaShawn Smith-Wright, Grover Easterling III, Joseph Verge, Golden, Maya Marshall, Ama Codjoe, Samiya Bashir, Alexis Pauline Gumbs, Aracelis Girmay, Victoria Chang, Aimee Nezhukumatathil, Hieu Minh Nguyen, Sam Smith, Paul Tran, Alison C. Rollins, Nate Marshall, Kemi Alabi, Courtney Faye Taylor, Camonghne Felix, Safia Elhillo, Ariana Benson, Lauren Bullock, Evie Shockley, Nicole Sealey, Luther Hughes, Sarah Ghazal Ali, Charlotte Abotsi, Shira Erlichman, Jericho Brown, Jason B. Crawford, Natasha Oladokun, Matthew Olzmann, Hanif Abdurraqib, Safiya Sinclair, I.S. Jones, Willie Lee Kinard III, Joy Priest, Kiese Laymon, and countless others.

For helping me better see myself: Toni Morrison, Ntozake Shange, Rita Dove, Natasha Trethewey, Wanda Coleman, Krista Franklin, Rachel Eliza Griffiths, June Jordan, Zora Neale Hurston, Saidiya Hartman, Toi Derricotte, Morgan Parker, Gwendolyn Brooks, and Vievee Francis.

I am grateful to have received such loving support from the following communities: Tin House Winter Workshop, InsideOut Literary Arts, and the *VS* podcast team. My Randolph MFA family: Gary Dop, Christopher Gaumer, and my faculty mentors, official and adopted. The Watering Hole, especially the 2019 Manuscript Fellows. Pink Door Writing Retreat. VONA, and the 2017 Twerkshop. Kresge Arts in Detroit, specifically Ebony Jones and the 2023 cohort of fellows and awardees. My Cass Tech family, especially the English Department. And of course, my sorors of Sigma Gamma Rho Sorority, Incorporated, especially my home chapter Delta Epsilon, and "The Crew."

Thank you to Tin House's amazing staff for championing my work so fiercely. Thank you to my blurbers for generously ushering *Good Dress* into the world. Thanks to Rachel Eliza Griffiths for allowing me use of your beautiful artwork. Thanks to Beth Steidle for making it into an amazing cover. Gratitude forever to kiki nicole: *Good Dress* would not be who she is without your careful eye and attention. Endless appreciation to the Detroit School—it is an honor to stand in your legacy. Angel, Airea, Aricka, and Phillip: for your friendship and your love.

Thank you to my forever loves: Ajanaé, you already know. Til' the wheels fall off and then some. Mars, for the way you love me, and allow me to love you back. Mick, for voice notes, and time, and so much tenderness. Justin, I literally could not do any of this without you. My children, for your love and patience. My matriarchy, especially Mommy and Granny, for absolutely everything.

Brittany Rogers is a poet, educator, and lifelong Detroiter. Her work has been published in *Prairie Schooner*, *Indiana Review*, Four Way Review, underbelly, *Mississippi Review*, Lambda Literary, Oprah Daily, and elsewhere. Brittany is a fellow of VONA, The Watering Hole, Poetry Incubator, and Pink Door Writing Retreat. She is editor in chief of Muzzle Magazine and co-host of VS podcast.